Elegant, Fashionable, Chic
ACCESSORIES
to Crochet™

Contents

DESERT SOUTHWEST
Scarf, Mitts & Headband

SCARF

SKILL LEVEL
■■□□
EASY

FINISHED MEASUREMENTS
5 x 60 inches

MATERIALS
■ Cascade Yarns Casablanca medium (worsted) weight wool/silk/mohair yarn (3½ oz/220 yds/100g per skein): 2 skeins #08 forest
■ Size I/9/5.5mm crochet hook or size needed to obtain gauge
■ Tapestry needle

GAUGE
14 sts = 4 inches; 16 rows = 4 inches

PATTERN NOTE
Weave in ends as work progresses.

SCARF
Row 1 (WS): Ch 18, sc in 2nd ch from hook, sc in each rem ch across, turn. *(17 sc)*

Row 2 (RS): Ch 1, sc in each st across, turn.

Row 3: Rep row 2.

Row 4: Ch 1, sc in first sc, **fpdc** *(see Stitch Guide)* around next sc on 2nd row below, *on working row, sc in next sc, fpdc around each of next 4 sc on 2nd row below, on working row, sc in next sc, fpdc around next sc on 2nd row below, rep from * once, on working row, sc in last sc, turn. *(11 fpdc, 6 sc)*

Row 5: Rep row 2.

Row 6: Ch 1, sc in first sc, fpdc around next fpdc on 2nd row below, *sc in next sc, fpdc around each of next 4 fpdc on 2nd row below, sc in next sc, fpdc around next fpdc on 2nd row below, rep from * once, sc in last sc, turn.

Row 7: Rep row 2.

Row 8: Ch 1, sc in first sc, fpdc around next fpdc on 2nd row below, *sc in next sc, sk next 2 fpdc on 2nd row below, **fptr** *(see Stitch Guide)* around each of next 2 fpdc, fptr around first sk fpdc, fptr around 2nd sk fpdc, sc in next sc, fpdc around next fpdc on 2nd row below, rep from * once, sc in last sc, turn.

Row 9: Rep row 2.

Row 10: Ch 1, sc in first sc, fpdc around fpdc on 2nd row below, *sc in next sc, fpdc around each of next 4 fptr on 2nd row below, sc in next sc, fpdc around next fpdc on 2nd row below, rep from * once, sc in last sc, turn.

Rows 11–238: [Rep rows 5–10 consecutively] 38 times.

Row 239: Rep row 5.

Row 240: Rep row 6. At end of row, do not turn.

EDGING
Working across next side in ends of rows, work 240 sc evenly sp across to next corner, 3 sc in corner, working across next side in unused lps of foundation ch, sc in each ch across to next corner, 3 sc in corner, working across next side in ends of rows, work 240 sc evenly sp across to next corner, 3 sc in corner, sc in each st across last row to next corner, 3 sc in corner, join with sl st in first sc. Fasten off.

MITTS

SKILL LEVEL

EASY

FINISHED SIZE
Adult woman

FINISHED MEASUREMENTS
7½ inches long x 8 inches in circumference

MATERIALS
- Cascade Yarns Casablanca medium (worsted) weight wool/silk/mohair yarn (3½ oz/220 yds/100g per skein): 1 skein #08 forest
- Size I/9/5.5mm crochet hook or size needed to obtain gauge
- Tapestry needle

GAUGE
14 sts = 4 inches; 16 rows = 4 inches

PATTERN NOTES
To have mitts work up in similar shading, wind skein half at a time. This will ensure a close shading match.

Weave in ends as work progresses.

Join with slip stitch as indicated unless otherwise stated.

LEFT MITT
Rnd 1 (WS): Ch 26, being careful not to twist ch, **join** (*see Pattern Notes*) in first ch to form ring, ch 1, sc in same ch as beg ch-1, sc in each rem ch around, join in first sc, turn. (*26 sc*)

Rnds 2 & 3: Ch 1, sc in same ch as beg ch-1, sc in each rem sc around, join in first sc, turn.

Rnd 4: Ch 1, sc in same sc as beg ch-1, sc in next sc, **fpdc** (*see Stitch Guide*) around next sc on 2nd rnd below, sc in each of next 3 sc, fpdc around each of next 4 sc on 2nd rnd below, sc in each of next 3 sc, fpdc around next sc on 2nd rnd below, sc in each rem sc, join in first sc, turn. (*6 fpdc, 20 sc*)

Rnd 5: Ch 1, sc in same sc as beg ch-1, sc in each rem sc around, join in first sc, turn.

Rnd 6: Ch 1, sc in same sc as beg ch-1, sc in next sc, fpdc around next fpdc on 2nd rnd below, sc in each of next 3 sc, fpdc around each of next 4 fpdc on 2nd rnd below, sc in each of next 3 sc, fpdc around next fpdc on 2nd rnd below, sc in each rem sc around, join in first sc, turn.

Rnd 7: Rep rnd 5.

Rnd 8: Ch 1, sc in same sc as beg ch-1, sc in next sc, fpdc around next fpdc on 2nd rnd below, sc in each of next 3 sc, sk next 2 fpdc on 2nd rnd below, **fptr** (*see Stitch Guide*) around each of next 2 fpdc, fptr around first sk fpdc, fptr around 2nd sk fpdc, sc in each of next 3 sc, fpdc around next fpdc on 2nd rnd below, sc in each rem sc around, join in first sc, turn.

Rnd 9: Rep rnd 5.

Rnd 10: Ch 1, sc in same sc as beg ch-1, sc in next sc, fpdc around next fpdc on 2nd rnd below, sc in each of next 3 sc, fpdc around each of next 4 fptr on 2nd rnd below, sc in each of next 3 sc, fpdc around next fpdc on 2nd rnd below, sc in each rem sc around, join in first sc, turn.

Rnds 11–14: [Rep rnds 5 and 6] twice.

Rnd 15: Rep rnd 5.

Row 16: Now working in rows, ch 1, sc in each of first 2 sc, fpdc around next fpdc on 2nd rnd below, sc in each of next 3 sc, sk next 2 fpdc on 2nd rnd below, fptr around each of next 2 fpdc, fptr around first sk fpdc, fptr around 2nd sk fpdc, sc in each of next 3 sc, fpdc around next fpdc on 2nd rnd below, sc in each rem sc across to last st, leaving last st unworked, turn. (*6 fpdc, 19 sc*)

Row 17: Ch 1, sc in each st across, turn.

Row 18: Ch 1, sc in each of first 2 sc, fpdc around next fpdc on 2nd row below, sc in each of next 3 sc, fpdc around each of next 4 fptr on 2nd row below, sc in each of next 3 sc, fpdc around next fpdc on 2nd row below, sc in each rem sc across, turn.

Row 19: Rep row 17.

Rnd 20: Now working in rnds, ch 1, sc in same sc as beg ch-1, sc in next sc, fpdc around next fpdc on 2nd row below, sc in each of next 3 sc, fpdc around each of next 4 fpdc on 2nd row below, sc in each of next 3 sc, fpdc around next fpdc on 2nd row below, sc in each rem sc across, ch 1, join in first sc, turn. *(6 fpdc, 20 sc)*

Rnd 21: Ch 1, sc in same sc as beg ch-1, sc in next ch-1 sp, sc in each rem sc around, join in first sc, turn.

Rnds 22–30: Rep rnds 6–14.

Rnds 31 & 32: Rep rnd 5. At end of last rnd, fasten off.

RIGHT MITT
Rnds 1–3: Rep rnds 1–3 of Left Mitt.

Rnd 4: Ch 1, sc in same sc as beg ch-1, sc in each of next 11 sc, fpdc around next fpdc on 2nd rnd below, sc in each of next 3 sc, fpdc around each of next 4 sc on 2nd rnd below, sc in each of next 3 sc, fpdc around next sc on 2nd rnd below, sc in each of last 2 sc, join in first sc, turn. *(6 fpdc, 20 sc)*

Rnd 5: Ch 1, sc in same sc as beg ch-1, sc in each rem sc around, join in first sc, turn.

Rnd 6: Ch 1, sc in same sc as beg ch-1, sc in each of next 11 sc, fpdc around next fpdc on 2nd rnd below, sc in each of next 3 sc, fpdc around each of next 4 fpdc on 2nd rnd below, sc in each of next 3 sc, fpdc around next fpdc on 2nd rnd below, sc in each of last 2 sc, join in first sc, turn.

Rnd 7: Rep rnd 5.

Rnd 8: Ch 1, sc in same sc as beg ch-1, sc in each of next 11 sc, fpdc around next fpdc on 2nd rnd below, sc in each of next 3 sc, sk next 2 fpdc on 2nd rnd below, fptr around each of next 2 fpdc, fptr around first sk fpdc, fptr around 2nd sk fpdc, sc in each of next 3 sc, fpdc around next fpdc on 2nd rnd below, sc in each of last 2 sc, join in first sc, turn.

Rnd 9: Rep rnd 5.

Rnd 10: Ch 1, sc in same sc as beg ch-1, sc in each of next 11 sc, fpdc around next fpdc on 2nd rnd below, sc in each of next 3 sc, fpdc around each of next 4 fptr on 2nd rnd below, sc in each of next 3 sc, fpdc around next fpdc on 2nd rnd below, sc in each of last 2 sc, join in first sc, turn.

Rnds 11–14: [Rep rnds 5 and 6] twice.

Rnd 15: Rep rnd 5.

Row 16: Now working in rows, ch 1, sc in each of first 12 sc, fpdc around next fpdc on 2nd rnd below, sc in each of next 3 sc, sk next 2 fpdc on 2nd rnd below, fptr around each of next 2 fptr, fpdc around first sk fpdc, fptr around 2nd sk fpdc, sc in each of next 3 sc, fpdc around next fpdc on 2nd rnd below, sc in next sc, leaving last st unworked, turn. *(6 fpdc, 19 sc)*

Row 17: Ch 1, sc in each st across, turn.

Row 18: Ch 1, sc in each of first 12 sc, fpdc around next fpdc on 2nd row below, sc in each of next 3 sc, fpdc around each of next 4 fptr on 2nd row below, sc in each of next 3 sc, fpdc around next fpdc on 2nd row below, sc in last sc, turn.

Row 19: Rep row 17.

Rnd 20: Now working in rnds, ch 1, sc in same sc as beg ch-1, sc in each of next 11 sc, fpdc around next fpdc on 2nd row below, sc in each of next 3 sc, fpdc around each of next 4 fpdc on 2nd row below, sc in each of next 3 sc, fpdc around next fpdc on 2nd row below, sc in last sc, ch 1, join in first sc, turn.

Rnd 21: Ch 1, sc in same sc as beg ch-1, sc in next ch-1 sp, sc in each rem sc around, join in first sc, turn.

Rnds 22–30: Rep rnds 6–14.

Rnds 31 & 32: Rep rnd 5. At end of last rnd, fasten off.

FINISHING
Lightly block to soften yarn.

HEADBAND

SKILL LEVEL

EASY

FINISHED SIZE
Adult woman

FINISHED MEASUREMENTS
3 inches wide x 20 inches in circumference

MATERIALS
- Cascade Yarns Casablanca medium (worsted) weight wool/silk/mohair yarn (3½ oz/220 yds/100g per skein): 1 skein #08 forest
- Size I/9/5.5mm crochet hook or size needed to obtain gauge
- Tapestry needle

GAUGE
14 sc = 4 inches; 16 rows = 4 inches

PATTERN NOTE
Weave in ends as work progresses.

HEADBAND
Row 1 (RS): Ch 11, sc in 2nd ch from hook, sc in each rem ch across, turn. *(10 sc)*

Row 2: Ch 1, sc in each st across, turn.

Row 3: Ch 1, sc in first sc, **fpdc** *(see Stitch Guide)* around next sc on 2nd row below, sc in next sc, fpdc around each of next 4 sc on 2nd row below, sc in next sc, fpdc around next sc on 2nd row below, sc in last sc, turn. *(6 fpdc, 4 sc)*

Row 4: Rep row 2.

Row 5: Ch 1, sc in first sc, fpdc around next fpdc on 2nd row below, sc in next sc, fpdc around each of next 4 fpdc on 2nd row below, sc in next sc, fpdc around next fpdc on 2nd row below, sc in last sc, turn.

Row 6: Rep row 2.

Row 7: Ch 1, sc in first sc, fpdc around next fpdc on 2nd row below, sc in next sc, sk next 2 fpdc on 2nd row below, **fptr** *(see Stitch Guide)* around each of next 2 fpdc on 2nd row below, fptr around each of 2 sk fpdc, sc in next sc, fpdc around next fpdc on 2nd row below, sc in last sc, turn.

Row 8: Rep row 2.

Row 9: Ch 1, sc in first sc, fpdc around next fpdc on 2nd row below, sc in next sc, fpdc around each of next 4 fptr on 2nd row below, sc in next sc, fpdc around next fpdc on 2nd row below, sc in last sc, turn.

Rows 10–75: [Rep rows 4–9 consecutively] 11 times.

Row 76: Ch 1, sc in each st across. Do not turn.

ASSEMBLY
Fold piece in half with RS of row 76 facing RS of foundation ch, working through both thicknesses at same time, ch 1, sl st in each st across.

Turn piece inside out so RS is facing out.

EDGING
Ch 1, working in ends of rows around long side, work 76 sc evenly sp around, join with sl st in first sc. Fasten off.

With RS facing, join yarn with sl st in seam on opposite long side, ch 1, sc in same place as beg ch-1, working in ends of rows around side, work 75 sc evenly sp around, join in first sc. Fasten off. ■

HEARTLAND
Hat, Scarf & Mitts

HAT

SKILL LEVEL

EASY

FINISHED SIZE
Adult man

FINISHED MEASUREMENTS
7 inches long (with brim folded up) x 22 inches in circumference

MATERIALS
- Cascade Yarns 220 Superwash medium (worsted) weight superwash wool yarn (3½ oz/220 yds/100g per skein): **4 MEDIUM**
    1 skein #863 cordavan
- Size I/9/5.5mm crochet hook or size needed to obtain gauge
- Tapestry needle

GAUGE
16 ext sc = 4 inches; 16 rows = 4 inches

PATTERN NOTES
Weave in ends as work progresses.
Join with slip stitch as indicated unless otherwise stated.

SPECIAL STITCHES
Extended single crochet (ext sc): Draw up lp in indicated st, yo, draw through 1 lp on hook, yo, draw through 2 lps on hook.
Extended single crochet decrease (ext sc dec): Draw up lp in first indicated st, yo, draw through 1 lp on hook, draw up lp in next st, yo, draw through 1 lp on hook, yo, draw through 3 lps on hook.

HAT
BRIM
Row 1 (WS): Ch 17, sc in 2nd ch from hook, sc in each rem ch across, turn. *(16 sc)*

Rows 2–86: Ch 1, working in **back lps** *(see Stitch Guide)*, sc in each sc across, turn.

Row 87: Bring row 1 behind work, working through both thicknesses at same time, ch 1, sl st in each st across. Do not fasten off.

Turn Brim inside out so seam is on inside.

CROWN
Rnd 1 (RS): Ch 1, work 86 sc evenly sp around long edge of Brim, **join** *(see Pattern Notes)* in first sc, turn. *(86 sc)*

Rnd 2: Ch 1, **ext sc** *(see Special Stitches)* in each st around, join in first st, turn.

Rnds 3–10: Rep rnd 2.

Rnd 11: Ch 1, ext sc in same st as beg ch-1, ext sc in each of next 11 sts, **ext sc dec** *(see Special Stitches)* in next 2 sts, [ext sc in each of next 12 sts, ext sc dec in next 2 sts] 5 times, ext sc in each of last 2 sts, join in first st, turn. *(80 ext sc)*

Rnd 12: Ch 1, ext sc in same st as beg ch-1, ext sc in each of next 5 sts, ext sc dec in next 2 sts, [ext sc in each of next 6 sts, ext sc dec in next 2 sts] 9 times, join in first st, turn. *(70 ext sc)*

Rnd 13: Ch 1, ext sc in same st as beg ch-1, ext sc in each of next 4 sts, ext sc dec in next 2 sts, [ext sc in each of next 5 sts, ext sc dec in next 2 sts] 9 times, join in first st, turn. *(60 ext sc)*

Rnd 14: Ch 1, ext sc in same st as beg ch-1, ext sc in each of next 3 sts, ext sc dec in next 2 sts, [ext sc in each of next 4 sts, ext sc dec in next 2 sts] 9 times, join in first st, turn. *(50 ext sc)*

Rnd 15: Ch 1, ext sc in same st as beg ch-1, ext sc in each of next 2 sts, ext sc dec in next 2 sts, [ext sc in each of next 3 sts, ext sc dec in next 2 sts] 9 times, join in first st, turn. *(40 ext sc)*

Rnd 16: Rep rnd 2.

Rnd 17: Ch 1, ext sc in same st as beg ch-1, ext sc in next st, ext sc dec in next 2 sts, [ext sc in each of next 2 sts, ext sc dec in next 2 sts] 9 times, join in first st, turn. *(30 ext sc)*

Rnd 18: Rep rnd 2.

Rnd 19: Ch 1, ext sc in same st as beg ch-1, ext sc dec in next 2 sts, [ext sc in next st, ext sc dec in next 2 sts] 9 times, join in first st, turn. *(20 ext sc)*

Rnd 20: Ch 1, **sc dec** *(see Stitch Guide)* in same st as beg ch-1 and next sc, [sc dec in next 2 sts] 9 times, join in first sc, turn. *(10 sts)*

Rnd 21: Ch 1, sc dec in same st as beg ch-1 and next sc, [sc dec in next 2 sts] 4 times, join in first sc. Leaving long tail, fasten off. *(5 sts)*

FINISHING
With tapestry needle, weave long tail through sts of rnd 21, gather to close opening and secure.

SCARF

SKILL LEVEL
■■□□
EASY

FINISHED MEASUREMENTS
4½ x 51½ inches

MATERIALS

- Cascade Yarns 220 Superwash medium (worsted) weight superwash wool yarn (3½ oz/220 yds/100g per skein): 1 skein #863 cordavan
- Size I/9/5.5mm crochet hook or size needed to obtain gauge
- Tapestry needle

GAUGE
14 hdc = 4 inches; 16 rows = 4 inches

PATTERN NOTES
Weave in ends as work progresses.
Join with slip stitch as indicated unless otherwise stated.

SCARF
Row 1 (WS): Ch 202, hdc in 3rd ch from hook, hdc in each rem ch across, turn. *(200 hdc)*

Rows 2–17: Ch 2, working in **back lps** *(see Stitch Guide)*, hdc in each st across, turn.

Row 18: Ch 2, working in back lps, hdc in each st across. **Do not turn.**

FIRST SIDE EDGING
Row 1 (RS): Working across next short side, work 27 sc evenly sp across side. **Do not turn.**

Row 2: Ch 1, working left to right, work **reverse sc** *(see Stitch Guide)* in each st across. Fasten off.

2ND SIDE EDGING
Row 1: Hold Scarf with opposite short side at top, **join** *(see Pattern Notes)* yarn in right-hand corner, ch 1, working across side, work 27 sc evenly sp across. **Do not turn.**

Row 2: Ch 1, working left to right, work reverse sc in each st across. Fasten off.

MITTS

SKILL LEVEL

EASY

FINISHED SIZE
Adult man

FINISHED MEASUREMENTS
8½ inches in circumference around palm,
  not including thumb
7 inches in length with shorter cuff
8 inches in length with longer cuff

MATERIALS
- Cascade Yarns 220 Superwash
  medium (worsted) weight superwash
  wool yarn (3½ oz/220 yds/100g per skein):
    1 skein #863 cordavan
- Size I/9/5.5mm crochet hook or size needed
  to obtain gauge
- Tapestry needle

GAUGE
16 ext sc = 4 inches; 16 rows = 4 inches

PATTERN NOTES
Weave in ends as work progresses.
Join with slip stitch as indicated unless otherwise
  stated.

SPECIAL STITCH
Extended single crochet (ext sc): Draw up lp in
  indicated st, yo, draw through 1 lp on hook, yo,
  draw through 2 lps on hook.

MITT
MAKE 2.
CUFF
Row 1 (WS): Ch 11 for shorter cuff (ch 15 for
  longer cuff), sc in 2nd ch from hook, sc in each
  rem ch across, turn.

Rows 2–32: Ch 1, working in **back lps** (see Stitch
  Guide), sc in each sc across, turn.

Row 33: Bring row 1 behind work, working
  through both thicknesses at same time, ch 1,
  sl st in each st across. Do not fasten off.

Turn cuff inside out so seam is on inside.

HAND
Rnd 1 (RS): Ch 1, working across long edge of
  Cuff, work 32 sc evenly sp around, **join** (see
  Pattern Notes) in first sc, turn. (32 sc)

Rnd 2: Ch 1, **ext sc** (see Special Stitch) in each st
  around, join in first st, turn.

Rnds 3 & 4: Rep rnd 2.

Rnd 5: Ch 1, ext sc in same st as beg ch-1, sc in
  each of next 14 sts, 2 ext sc in each of next 2 sts,
  ext sc in each of last 15 sts, join in first st, turn.
  (34 sts)

Rnd 6: Ch 1, ext sc in same st as beg ch-1, ext sc
  in each of next 15 sts, 2 ext sc in each of next
  2 sts, ext sc in each of last 16 sts, join in first st,
  turn. (36 sts)

Rnds 7 & 8: Rep rnd 2.

Rnd 9: Ch 1, ext sc in same st as beg ch-1, ext sc
  in each of next 13 sts, ch 1, sk next 7 sts (thumb
  opening), ext sc in each of last 15 sts, join in first
  st, turn. (30 sts)

Rnd 10: Ch 1, ext sc in same st as beg ch-1, ext sc
  in each of next 14 sts, ext sc in next ch, ext sc in
  each of last 14 sts, join in first st, turn. (30 sts)

Rnds 11 & 12: Rep rnd 2.

PINKIE FINGER

Rnd 1: Ch 1, ext sc in same st as beg ch-1, ext sc in each of next 2 sts, ch 2, sk next 23 sts, ext sc in each of last 4 sts, join in first st, turn. *(9 sts)*

Rnd 2: Ch 1, ext sc in same st as beg ch-1, ext sc in each of next 3 sts, ext sc in each of next 2 chs, ext sc in each of last 3 sts, join in first st, turn. *(9 sts)*

Rnd 3: Ch 1, ext sc in same st as beg ch-1, ext sc in each rem st around, join in first st. Fasten off.

RING FINGER

Rnd 1: With RS facing and thumb opening on left, join yarn in first sk st from Pinkie Finger, ch 1, ext sc in same st as beg ch-1, ext sc in each of next 3 sts, ch 2, sk next 16 sts, ext sc in each of last 3 sts, ext sc in each of next 2 chs at base of Pinkie Finger, join in first st, turn.

Rnd 2: Ch 1, ext sc in same st as beg ch-1, ext sc in each of next 4 sts, ext sc in each of next 2 chs, ext sc in each of last 4 sts, join in first st, turn. *(11 sts)*

Rnds 3 & 4: Ch 1, ext sc in same st as beg ch-1, ext sc in each rem st around, join in first st. At end of last rnd, fasten off.

MIDDLE FINGER

Rnd 1: With RS facing and thumb opening on left, join yarn in first sk st from Ring Finger, ch 1, ext sc in same st as beg ch-1, ext sc in each of next 2 sts, ch 2, sk next 9 sts, ext sc in each of last 4 sts, ext sc in each of next 2 chs at base of Ring Finger, join in first st, turn.

Rnd 2: Ch 1, ext sc in same st as beg ch-1, ext sc in each of next 5 sts, ext sc in each of next 2 chs, ext sc in each of last 3 sts, join in first st, turn. *(11 sts)*

Rnds 3 & 4: Ch 1, ext sc in same st as beg ch-1, ext sc in each rem st around, join in first st. At end of last rnd, fasten off.

INDEX FINGER

Rnd 1: With RS facing and thumb opening on left, join yarn in first sk st from Middle Finger, ch 1, ext sc in same st as beg ch-1, ext sc in each of next 9 sts, ext sc in each of next 2 chs at base of Middle Finger, join in first st, turn.

Rnds 2–4: Ch 1, ext sc in same st as beg ch-1, ext sc in each rem st around, join in first st. At end of last rnd, fasten off.

THUMB

Rnd 1 (RS): With RS facing and thumb opening on left, join yarn in corner of thumb opening, ch 1, ext sc in same st as beg ch-1, ext sc in each of next 7 sts, ext sc in other corner of thumb opening, ext sc in next ch, join in first st, turn. *(10 sts)*

Rnds 2–4: Ch 1, ext sc in same st as beg ch-1, ext sc in each rem st around, join in first st. At end of last rnd, fasten off. ∎

PURPLE MOUNTAIN
Hat & Mitts

HAT

SKILL LEVEL

EASY

FINISHED SIZE
Adult woman

FINISHED MEASUREMENTS
12 inches long x 22 inches in circumference

MATERIALS
- Cascade Yarns Casablanca medium (worsted) weight wool/silk/mohair yarn (3½ oz/220 yds/100g per skein): 1 skein #03 galah cockatoo
- Size I/9/5.5mm crochet hook or size needed to obtain gauge
- Tapestry needle

MEDIUM 4

GAUGE
14 sc = 4 inches; 12 rows = 4 inches

PATTERN NOTES
Weave in ends as work progresses.
Join with slip stitch as indicated unless otherwise stated.
Chain-4 at beginning of round counts as first double crochet and chain-1 unless otherwise stated.

HAT
Rnd 1 (RS): Ch 60, being careful not to twist ch, **join** (see Pattern Notes) in first ch to form ring, ch 1, sc in same ch as beg ch-1, sc in each rem ch around, join in first sc, turn. (60 sc)

Rnd 2: Ch 1, sc in same sc as beg ch-1, dc in next sc, *sc in next sc, dc in next sc, rep from * around, join in first sc, turn.

Rnds 3–21: Ch 1, sc in same dc as beg ch-1, dc in next sc, *sc in next dc, dc in next sc, rep from * around, join in first sc, turn.

Rnd 22: Ch 1, sc in same dc as beg ch-1, *(dc, sc) in each of next 2 sts, [dc in next sc, sc in next dc] 9 times, rep from * once, (dc, sc) in each of next 2 sts, [dc in next sc, sc in next dc] 8 times, dc in last sc, join in first sc, turn. (66 sts)

Rnd 23: Ch 1, sc in same dc as beg ch-1, dc in next sc, *[sc in next dc, dc in next sc] 11 times, (sc, dc) in each of next 2 sts, *[sc in next dc, dc in next sc] 12 times, (sc, dc) in each of next 2 sts, rep from * once, join in first sc, turn. (72 sts)

Rnd 24: Ch 4 (see Pattern Notes), *sk next dc, dc in next sc, ch 1, rep from * around, join in 3rd of beg ch-4, turn. (36 ch sps)

Rnd 25: Ch 1, sc in same st as beg ch-1, dc in next ch-1 sp, *sc in next dc, dc in next ch-1 sp, rep from * around, join in first sc, turn. (72 sts)

Rnd 26: Ch 1, sc in same dc as beg ch-1, dc in next sc, [sc in next dc, dc in next sc] 10 times, (sc, dc) in each of next 2 sts, *[sc in next dc, dc in next sc] 11 times, (sc, dc) in each of next 2 sts, rep from * once, join in first sc, turn. (78 sts)

Rnds 27–30: Rep rnd 3.

TOP EDGING
Rnd 1 (RS): Ch 1, sc in same st as beg ch-1, sk next 2 sts, 3 dc in next st, sk next st, sc in next st, sk next 2 sts, 3 dc in next st, sk next st, *sc in next st, sk next st, 3 dc in next st, sk next st, rep from * around, join in first sc. Fasten off. (57 dc, 19 sc)

BOTTOM EDGING

Rnd 1 (RS): Hold piece with RS facing and foundation ch at top, join yarn in unused lp of first ch of foundation ch, ch 1, sc in same lp as beg ch-1, *sk next ch, 3 dc in next ch, sk next ch**, sc in next ch, rep from * around, ending last rep at **, join in first sc. Fasten off. *(45 dc, 15 sc)*

CORD

Ch 121, sc in 2nd ch from hook, sc in each rem ch across. Fasten off. *(120 sc)*

FINISHING

Thread Cord through ch-1 sps of rnd 24 and tie in bow.

MITTENS

SKILL LEVEL

EASY

FINISHED SIZE

Adult woman

FINISHED MEASUREMENTS

10 inches long x 8 inches around palm

MATERIALS

- Cascade Yarns Casablanca medium (worsted) weight wool/silk/mohair yarn (3½ oz/220 yds/100g per skein): 1 skein #03 galah cockatoo
- Size I/9/5.5mm crochet hook or size needed to obtain gauge
- Tapestry needle

4 MEDIUM

GAUGE

14 sc = 4 inches; 12 rows = 4 inches

PATTERN NOTES

Weave in ends as work progresses.
To have mittens work up in similar shading, wind skein half at a time. This will ensure a close shading match.
Join with slip stitch as indicated unless otherwise stated.

MITTEN
MAKE 2.
CUFF

Row 1: Ch 11, sc in 2nd ch from hook, sc in each rem ch across, turn. *(10 sc)*

Rows 2–24: Ch 1, working in **back lps** *(see Stitch Guide)*, sc in each sc across, turn.

Row 25: Bring row 1 behind row 24, working through both thicknesses at same time, ch 1, sc in each st across. Do not fasten off.

Turn Cuff inside out so seam is on inside.

HAND

Rnd 1 (RS): Ch 1, working around long side of Cuff, work 26 sc evenly sp around, **join** *(see Pattern Notes)* in first sc, turn. *(26 sc)*

Rnd 2: Ch 1, sc in same sc as beg ch-1, dc in next sc, *sc in next sc, dc in next sc, rep from * around, join in first sc, turn.

Rnd 3: Ch 1, sc in same st as beg ch-1, dc in next st, [sc in next st, dc in next st] 5 times, (sc, dc) in each of next 2 sts, [sc in next st, dc in next st] 6 times, join in first sc, turn. *(28 sts)*

Rnd 4: Ch 1, sc in same st as beg ch-1, dc in next st, [sc in next st, dc in next st] 5 times, sc in next st, (dc, sc) in each of next 2 sts, dc in next st, [sc in next st, dc in next st] 6 times, join in first sc, turn. *(30 sts)*

Rnd 5: Ch 1, sc in same st as beg ch-1, dc in next st, [sc in next st, dc in next st] 6 times, (sc, dc) in each of next 2 sts, [sc in next st, dc in next st] 7 times, join in first sc, turn. *(32 sts)*

Rnd 6: Ch 1, *sc in next dc, dc in next sc, rep from * around, join in first sc, turn.

Rnds 7–9: Ch 1, *sc in next dc, dc in next sc, rep from * around, join in first sc, turn.

Rnd 10: Ch 1, sc in same st as beg ch-1, dc in next st, [sc in next st, dc in next st] 5 times, ch 2, sk next 8 sts *(thumb opening)*, [sc in next st, dc in next st] 6 times, join in first sc, turn. *(24 sts, 1 ch-2 sp)*

Rnd 11: Ch 1, sc in same st as beg ch-1, dc in next st, [sc in next st, dc in next st] 5 times, sc in next ch, dc in next ch, [sc in next st, dc in next st] 6 times, join in first sc, turn. *(26 sts)*

Rnds 12–16: Rep rnd 6.

Rnd 17: Ch 1, **sc dec** *(see Stitch Guide)* in same st as beg ch-1 and next st, **dc dec** *(see Stitch Guide)* in next 2 sts, *sc in next st, dc in next st, rep from * around, join in first sc, turn. *(24 sts)*

Rnd 18: Ch 1, sc in same st as beg ch-1, dc in next st, [sc in next st, dc in next st] 4 times, sc dec in next 2 sts, dc dec in next 2 sts, *sc in next st, dc in next st, rep from * around, join in first sc, turn. *(22 sts)*

Rnds 19 & 20: Rep rnd 6.

Rnd 21: Rep rnd 17. *(20 sts)*

Rnd 22: Rep rnd 6.

Rnd 23: Ch 1, sc in same st as beg ch-1, dc in next st, [sc in next st, dc in next st] 3 times, sc dec in next 2 sts, dc dec in next 2 sts, *sc in next st, dc in next st, rep from * around, join in first sc, turn. *(18 sts)*

Rnd 24: Ch 1, sc dec in same st as beg ch-1 and in next st, [sc dec in next 2 sts] 8 times, join in first st, turn. *(9 sts)*

Rnd 25: Ch 1, sc in same st as beg ch-1, [sc dec in next 2 sts] 4 times, join in first sc. Leaving long tail, fasten off. *(5 sts)*

FINISHING
With tapestry needle, weave long tail through sts of last rnd, gather to close opening and secure.

THUMB
Rnd 1 (RS): With RS facing and thumb opening on left, join yarn in corner of thumb opening, ch 1, sc in same st, [dc in next sc, sc in next dc] 4 times, dc in next corner of thumb opening, sc in next ch, dc in next ch, join in first sc, turn. *(12 sts)*

Rnds 2–6: Ch 1, sc in same st as beg ch-1, dc in next st, *sc in next st, dc in next st, rep from * around, join in first sc, turn.

Rnd 7: Ch 1, sc dec in same st as beg ch-1 and in next st, [sc dec in next 2 sts] 5 times, join in first st. Leaving long tail, fasten off. *(6 sts)*

FINISHING
With tapestry needle, weave long tail through sts of rnd 25 of Hand, gather to close opening and secure. In same manner, weave long tail through sts of rnd 7 of Thumb, gather to close opening and secure. ∎

METRO
Headwrap & Gloves

HEADWRAP

SKILL LEVEL

EASY

FINISHED MEASUREMENTS
60 inches wide x 20½ inches long; 20¾ inches around hood

MATERIALS
- Cascade Yarns Heritage 150 fine weight superwash wool/nylon yarn (5¼ oz/492 yds/150g per skein): 2 skeins #5601 night
- Size E/4/3.5mm crochet hook or size needed to obtain gauge
- Tapestry needle
- Beading needle large enough for yarn
- Size 0/6 silver-lined seed beads: 36

② FINE

GAUGE
18 dc = 4 inches; 13 rows = 4 inches

PATTERN NOTES
Weave in ends as work progresses.

Chain-5 at beginning of row counts as first double crochet and chain-2 space unless otherwise stated.

Chain-3 at beginning of row counts as first double crochet unless otherwise stated.

Join with slip stitch as indicated unless otherwise stated.

SPECIAL STITCH
Bead single crochet (bead sc): Push bead close to hook, sc in indicated st.

HEADWRAP
NECK WRAP
Row 1 (RS): Ch 270, dc in 4th ch from hook (*3 sk chs count as a dc*), dc in each rem ch across, turn. (*268 dc*)

Row 2: Ch 1, sc in first dc, *ch 4, sk next 2 sc, sc in next dc, rep from * across to last st, sc in 3rd ch of beg 3 sk chs. (*89 ch sps*)

Row 3: Ch 5 (*see Pattern Notes*), sc in next ch-4 sp, *ch 4, sc in next ch-4 sp, rep from * across to last st, ch 2, dc in last st, turn.

Row 4: Ch 1, sc in first dc, *ch 4, sc in next ch-4 sp, rep from * across to last st, ch 4, sc in 3rd ch of beg ch-5, turn.

Row 5: Ch 3 (*see Pattern Notes*), 3 dc in each ch-4 sp across, turn. (*268 dc*)

Row 6: Ch 3, dc in next dc, *ch 1, sk next dc, dc in each of next 2 dc, rep from * across to last 2 sts, ch 1, sk next dc, dc in last st. (*179 dc*)

Row 7: Ch 3, dc in each ch-1 sp and dc across, turn. (*268 dc*)

Rows 8–19: [Rep rows 2–7 consecutively] twice. At end of last row, fasten off.

HOOD
Row 1 (WS): With WS facing, sk 88 sts on last row of Neck Wrap, **join** (*see Pattern Notes*) yarn in next st, ch 1, sc in same st as beg ch-1, [ch 4, sk next 2 sts, sc in next st] 30 times, turn. (*30 ch sps*)

Row 2: Ch 5, sc in next ch-4 sp, *ch 4, sc in next ch-4 sp, rep from * across to last st, ch 2, dc in last st, turn.

Row 3: Ch 1, sc in first dc, *ch 4, sc in next ch-4 sp, rep from * to end, working last sc in last st, turn.

Row 4: Ch 3, 3 dc in each ch-4 sp across, turn. *(91 sts)*

Row 5: Ch 3, dc in next st, *ch 1, sk next st, dc in each of next 2 sts, rep from * across to last 2 sts, ch 1, sk next st, dc in last st, turn. *(61 sts)*

Row 6: Ch 3, dc in each ch-1 sp and dc across, turn. *(91 dc)*

Row 7: Ch 1, sc in first dc, *ch 4, sk next 2 sc, sc in next dc, rep from * to end, working last sc in last st. *(30 sps)*

Rows 8–43: [Rep rows 2–7 consecutively] 6 times.

Rows 44–47: Rep rows 2–5.

Row 48: Ch 3, [**dc dec** *(see Stitch Guide)* in next 2 sts] 10 times, dc in each rem dc across. *(81 sts)*

ASSEMBLY
With WS facing, fold Hood in half, working through both thicknesses at same time, sl st in each st across. Fasten off.

HOOD EDGING
Row 1 (RS): With RS facing, join yarn to bottom outer corner of Hood, ch 1, work 175 sc evenly sp around hood edge, turn. *(175 sc)*

Row 2: Ch 1, sc in first sc, *ch 4, sk next 2 sc, sc in next sc, rep from * across. Fasten off.

BEADED NECK WRAP EDGING
Note: With beading needle, string 18 beads on yarn.

Row 1 (RS): With RS facing and 1 short end of Neck Wrap at top, join yarn at right-hand corner, ch 1, work 35 sc evenly sp across edge, turn. *(35 sc)*

Row 2: Ch 1, **bead sc** *(see Special Stitch)* in first sc, *sc in each of next 2 sc, bead sc in next sc, rep from * across to last sc, sc in last sc. Fasten off.

Thread rem beads on yarn and work Neck Wrap Edging in same manner on rem short end of Neck Wrap.

GLOVES

SKILL LEVEL

EASY

FINISHED SIZE
Adult woman

FINISHED MEASUREMENTS
7½ inches around palm, not including thumb
10½ inches in length to top of middle finger

MATERIALS

- Cascade Yarns Heritage 150 fine weight superwash wool/nylon yarn (5¼ oz/492 yds/150g per skein): 2 skeins #5601 night
- Size D/3/3.25mm crochet hook or size needed to obtain gauge
- Size 8/1.50mm steel crochet hook
- Tapestry needle
- Size 0/6 silver-lined seed beads: 80

GAUGE
22 sc = 4 inches; 28 rows = 4 inches

PATTERN NOTES
Weave in ends as work progresses.
Join with slip stitch as indicated unless otherwise stated.

SPECIAL STITCH
Bead single crochet (bead sc): Place bead on steel hook, remove lp on larger hook, with steel hook pull lp through bead, replace lp on larger hook, sc in indicated st.

GLOVE
MAKE 2.
CUFF
Row 1 (RS): Ch 15, sc in 2nd ch from hook, sc in each rem ch across, turn. *(14 sc)*

Row 2: Ch 1, working in **back lps** *(see Stitch Guide)*, sc in each sc across, working **bead sc** *(see Special Stitch)* in 2 evenly sp sc, turn.

Row 3: Ch 1, working in back lps, sc in each st across, turn.

Rows 4–41: [Rep rows 2 and 3 alternately] 19 times.

Row 42: Bring row 1 behind work, working through both thicknesses at same time, ch 1, sl st in each st across. Do not fasten off.

Turn Cuff inside out so seam is on inside.

HAND

Rnd 1 (RS): Ch 1, working around long edge of Cuff, work 40 sc evenly sp around, **join** (*see Pattern Notes*) in first sc, turn.

Rnds 2 & 3: Ch 1, sc in each sc around, join in first sc, turn.

Rnds 4–18: Ch 1, sc same st as beg ch-1, sc in each of next 18 sc, 2 sc in next sc, sc in each rem sc around, join in first sc, turn. (*55 sc*)

Rnd 19: Ch 1, sc in same st as beg ch-1, sc in each of next 35 sc, ch 2, count back 14 sc from hook and sl st in 15th sc, turn. Do not fasten off.

THUMB

Rnd 1 (WS): Ch 1, sc in each of the next 2 chs, sc in each of next 14 sc, join in first sc, turn. (*16 sc*)

Rnd 2: Ch 1, sc in each sc around, join in first sc, turn.

Rnds 3 & 4: Rep rnd 2.

Rnd 5 (for left Glove only): Ch 1, sc in same st as beg ch-1, sc in each of next 8 sc, sk next 7 sc, join in first sc, turn.

Rnd 5 (for right Glove only): Ch 1, sc in same st as beg ch-1, ch 7, sk next 7 sc, sc in each of next 8 sc, join in first sc, turn.

Rnd 6: Ch 1, sc in each ch and sc around, join in first sc, turn. (*16 sc*)

Rnds 7–13: Rep rnd 2.

Rnd 14: Ch 1, **sc dec** (*see Stitch Guide*) in same st as beg ch-1 and next st, [sc dec in next 2 sts] 7 times, join in first st. Leaving long tail, fasten off.

REMAINDER OF HAND

Rnd 1: With RS facing and thumb on right, join yarn at base of thumb, ch 1, sc in each of next 19 sc, join in first sc of rnd 19 of Hand.

Rnd 2: Ch 1, sc in same st as beg ch-1, sc in each of next 18 st, [sc dec in next 2 sts, sc in next st, sc dec in next 2 sts] across base of Thumb, sc in each of next 20 sc, join in first sc, turn. (*42 sc*)

Rnds 3–14: Ch 1, sc in each sc around, join in first sc, turn.

PINKIE FINGER

Rnd 1 (RS): Ch 1, sc in same st as beg ch-1, sc in each of next 6 sc, ch 4, sk next 31 sc, sc in each of last 4 sc, join in first sc, turn. *(11 sc, 1 ch-4 sp)*

Rnd 2: Ch 1, sc in each ch and sc around, join in first sc, turn. *(15 sc)*

Rnds 3–11: Ch 1, sc in each sc around, join in first sc, turn.

Rnd 12: Ch 1, sc in same st as beg ch-1, [sc dec in next 2 sts] 7 times, join in first st. Leaving long tail, fasten off.

RING FINGER

Rnd 1 (RS): With RS facing and thumb on left, join yarn in first sk st from Pinkie Finger, ch 1, sc in same st as beg ch-1, sc in each of next 4 sc, ch 3, sk next 21 sc, sc in each of next 5 sc, sc in each of next 4 chs across base of Pinkie Finger, join in first sc, turn. *(14 sc, 1 ch-3 sp)*

Rnd 2: Ch 1, sc in each ch and sc around, join in first sc, turn. (17 sc)

Rnds 3–17: Ch 1, sc in each st around, join in first sc, turn.

Rnd 18: Ch 1, sc in same st as beg ch-1, [sc dec in next 2 sts] 8 times, join in first st. Leaving long tail, fasten off.

MIDDLE FINGER

Rnd 1 (RS): With RS facing and thumb on left, join yarn in first sk st from Ring Finger, ch 1, sc in same st as beg ch-1, sc in each of next 4 sc, ch 5, sk next 11 sc, sc in each of next 5 sc, sc in each of next 3 chs across base of Ring Finger, join in first sc, turn. *(13 sc, 1 ch-5 sp)*

Rnd 2: Ch 1, sc in each sc and in ch around, join in first sc. *(18 sc)*

Rnds 3–19: Ch 1, sc in each sc around, join in first sc, turn.

Rnd 20: Ch 1, sc dec in same sc as beg ch-1 and next sc, [sc dec in next 2 sts] 8 times, join in first st. Leaving long tail, fasten off. *(9 sc)*

INDEX FINGER

Rnd 1 (RS): With RS facing and thumb on left, join yarn in first sk st after Middle Finger, ch 1, sc in each of next 11 sc, sc in unused lp of each of next 5 chs across base of Middle Finger, join in first sc, turn. *(16 sc)*

Rnd 2: Ch 1, sc in each sc around, join in first sc, turn.

Rnds 3–8: Rep rnd 2.

Rnd 9 (for right Glove only): Ch 1, sc in same sc as beg ch-1, sc in each of next 7 sc, ch 7, sk next 7 sc, sc in last sc, join in first sc, turn. *(9 sc, 1 ch-7 sp)*

Rnd 9 (for left Glove only): Ch 1, sc in same sc as beg ch-1, ch 7, sk next 7 sc, sc in each of last 8 sc, join in first sc, turn. *(9 sc, 1 ch-7 sp)*

Rnd 10: Ch 1, sc in each ch and sc around, join in first sc, turn. *(16 sc)*

Rnds 11–17: Rep rnd 2.

Rnd 18: Ch 1, sc dec in same sc as beg ch-1 and next sc, [sc dec in next 2 sc] 7 times, join in first st. Leaving long tail, fasten off. *(8 sc)*

FINISHING

With tapestry needle, weave long tails through sts of last rnd of each finger, gather to close opening and secure. ∎

PACIFIC NORTHWEST
Hat, Gloves & Scarf

HAT

SKILL LEVEL

EASY

FINISHED SIZE
Adult woman

FINISHED MEASUREMENTS
8¾ inches long x 20 inches in circumference

MATERIALS
- Cascade Yarns 220 Superwash Sport sport weight superwash wool yarn (1¾ oz/136 yds/50g per skein): 1 skein #893 ruby
- Size H/8/5mm crochet hook or size needed to obtain gauge
- Tapestry needle
- Sewing needle
- ⅞-inch buttons: 3
- Matching sewing thread

GAUGE
18 sc = 4 inches; 24 rows = 4 inches in ribbing

PATTERN NOTES
Weave in ends as work progresses.
Join with slip stitch as indicated unless otherwise stated.

HAT
BRIM
Row 1 (WS): Ch 91, sc in 2nd ch from hook, sc in each rem ch across, turn. *(90 sc)*

Rows 2–16: Ch 1, working in **back lps** *(see Stitch Guide)*, sc in each sc across, turn.

Row 17: Ch 1, working in back lps, sc in each sc across. Do not turn.

BUTTON PANEL
Row 1 (WS): Ch 1, working across next side in ends of rows, work 16 sc evenly sp across, turn.

Rows 2–4: Ch 1, sc in each sc across, turn. At end of last row, fasten off.

BUTTONHOLE PANEL

Row 1 (WS): With WS facing and unworked short side at top, **join** (*see Pattern Notes*) yarn in right-hand corner, ch 1, working across side in ends of rows, work 16 sc evenly sp across, turn.

Row 2: Ch 1, sc in each sc across, turn.

Row 3: Ch 1, sc in each of first 3 sc, *ch 2 (*buttonhole made*), sk next 2 sc, sc in each of next 2 sc, rep from * twice, sc in last sc, turn.

Row 4: Ch 1, sc in each of first 3 sc, *2 sc in next ch-2 sp, sc in each of next 2 sc, rep from * twice, sc in last sc. **Do not turn.**

CROWN

Rnd 1 (RS): Now working in rnds around outer edge of Brim, ch 1, work 3 sc evenly sp across Buttonhole Panel, working across next side, sc in back lp of each of next 90 sc, working across next side, work 3 sc evenly sp across Button Panel, sk first 3 sc of rnd, join in next sc. (*93 sc*)

Rnd 2: Ch 1, *sk next sc, 2 sc in next sc, rep from *around, join in first sc. (*92 sc*)

Rnds 3–13: Ch 1, sk same sc as beg ch-1, 2 sc in next sc, *sk next sc, 2 sc in next sc, rep from *around, join in first sc.

Rnd 14: Ch 1, sk same sc as beg ch-1, 2 sc in next sc, [sk next sc, 2 sc in next sc] 5 times, [**sc dec** (*see Stitch Guide*) in next 2 sts] twice, *[sk next sc, 2 sc in next sc] 6 times,[sc dec in next 2 sts] twice, rep from *3 times, [sk next sc, 2 sc in next sc] 4 times, [sc dec in next 2 sts] twice, join in first sc. (*80 sc*)

Rnd 15: Rep rnd 2.

Rnd 16: Ch 1, sk same sc as beg ch-1, 2 sc in next sc, *[sk next sc, 2 sc in next sc] 5 times, [sc dec in next 2 sts] twice, rep from * around, join in first sc. (*70 sc*)

Rnd 17: Rep rnd 2.

Rnd 18: Ch 1, sk same sc as beg ch-1, 2 sc in next sc, *[sk next sc, 2 sc in next sc] 3 times, [sc dec in next 2 sts] twice, rep from * around, join in first sc. (*60 sc*)

Rnd 19: Rep rnd 2.

Rnd 20: Ch 1, sk same sc as beg ch-1, 2 sc in next sc, *[sk next sc, 2 sc in next sc] 3 times, rep from * around, join in first sc. (*50 sc*)

Rnd 21: Rep rnd 2.

Rnd 22: Ch 1, sk same sc as beg ch-1, 2 sc in next sc, *[sk next sc, 2 sc in next sc] twice, [sc dec in next 2 sts] twice, rep from * around, join in first sc. (*40 sc*)

Rnd 23: Rep rnd 2.

Rnd 24: Ch 1, sk same sc as beg ch-1, 2 sc in next sc, sk next sc, 2 sc in next sc, [sc dec in next 2 sts] twice, *[sk next sc, 2 sc in next sc] twice, [sc dec in next 2 sts] twice, rep from * around, join in first sc. (*30 sc*)

Rnd 25: Ch 1, sk same as beg ch-1, 2 sc in next sc, [sc dec in next 2 sts] twice, *sk next sc, 2 sc in next sc, [sc dec in next 2 sts] twice, rep from * around, join in first sc. (*20 sc*)

Rnd 26: Ch 1, sc dec in same st as beg ch-1 and next sc, [sc dec in next 2 sts] 9 times, join in first sc. (*10 sc*)

Rnd 27: Ch 1, sc dec in same st as beg ch-1 and next sc, [sc dec in next 2 sts] 4 times, join in first sc. Leaving long tail, fasten off. (*5 sc*)

FINISHING

With tapestry needle, weave long tail through sts of rnd 17, gather to close opening and secure.

Sew buttons to Button Panel opposite buttonholes.

FINGERLESS GLOVES

SKILL LEVEL

EASY

FINISHED SIZE
Adult woman

FINISHED MEASUREMENTS
8 inches long x 7 inches in circumference around palm, not including thumb

MATERIALS
- Cascade Yarns 220 Superwash Sport sport weight superwash wool yarn (1¾ oz/136 yds/50g per skein): 1 skein #893 ruby
- Size H/8/5mm crochet hook or size needed to obtain gauge
- Tapestry needle
- Sewing needle
- ¾-inch buttons: 4
- Matching sewing thread

GAUGE
18 sc = 4 inches; 24 rows = 4 inches in ribbing

PATTERN NOTES
Weave in ends as work progresses.
Join with slip stitch as indicated unless otherwise stated.

LEFT GLOVE
CUFF
Row 1 (RS): Ch 29, sc in 2nd ch from hook, sc in each rem ch across, turn. *(28 sc)*

Rows 2–9: Ch 1, working in **back lps** *(see Stitch Guide)*, sc in each sc across, turn.

Row 10: Ch 1, working in back lps, sc in each sc across. Do not turn.

BUTTON PANEL
Row 1 (WS): Ch 1, working across next side in ends of rows, work 10 sc evenly sp across, turn.

Row 2: Ch 1, sc in each sc across, turn.

Row 3: Rep row 2.

Row 4: Ch 1, sc in each sc across, working across next long side of Cuff, ch 1, sc in end of each row of Button Panel, working in back lps, sc in each sc of row 10 of Cuff. Do not fasten off.

BUTTONHOLE PANEL
Row 1 (RS): Ch 1, working across next side in ends of rows, work 10 sc evenly sp across side, turn.

Row 2: Ch 1, sc in each sc across, turn.

Row 3: Ch 1, sc in each of first 2 sc, *ch 2 *(buttonhole made)*, sk next 2 sc, sc in each of next 2 sc, rep from * once, turn.

Row 4: Ch 1, sc in each of first 2 sc, *2 sc in next ch-2 sp, sc in each of next 2 sc, rep from * once, ch 1, working in ends of rows of Buttonhole Panel, sc in each row, turn to RS, **join** *(see Pattern Notes)* in first sc at top of Button Panel.

HAND
Rnd 1: Ch 1, sc in each sc around, join in first sc. *(32 sc)*

Rnd 2: Ch 1, sk same sc as beg ch-1, 2 sc in next sc, *sk next sc, 2 sc in next sc, rep from * around, join in first sc.

Rnd 3: Ch 1, sk same sc as beg ch-1, 2 sc in next sc, [sk next sc, 2 sc in next sc] 7 times, 2 sc in each of next 4 sc, [sk next sc, 2 sc in next sc] 6 times, join in first sc. *(36 sc)*

Rnd 4: Rep rnd 2.

Rnd 5: Ch 1, sk same sc as beg ch-1, 2 sc in next sc, [sk next sc, 2 sc in next sc] 8 times, 2 sc in each of next 4 sc, [sk next sc, 2 sc in next sc] 7 times, join in first sc. *(40 sc)*

Rnd 6: Rep rnd 2.

Rnd 7: Ch 1, sk same sc as beg ch-1, 2 sc in next sc, [sk next sc, 2 sc in next sc] 9 times, 2 sc in each of next 4 sc, [sk next sc, 2 sc in next sc] 8 times, join in first sc. *(44 sc)*

Rnds 8–14: Rep rnd 2.

Rnd 15: Ch 1, sk same sc as beg ch-1, 2 sc in next sc, [sk next sc, 2 sc in next sc] 7 times, ch 4, sk next 11 sc *(thumb opening made)*, 2 sc in next sc, [sk next sc, 2 sc in next sc] 8 times, join in first sc. *(38 sts)*

Rnd 16: Ch 1, sk same sc as beg ch-1, 2 sc in next sc, [sk next sc, 2 sc in next sc] 7 times, [sk next ch, 2 sc in next ch] twice, [sk next sc, 2 sc in next sc] 9 times, join in first sc. *(38 sc)*

Rnds 17–22: Rep rnd 2.

PINKIE FINGER
Rnd 1: Ch 1, sk same sc as beg ch-1, 2 sc in next sc, sk next sc, 2 sc in next sc, ch 4, sk next 31 sc, 2 sc in next sc, sk next sc, 2 sc in last sc, join in first sc. *(12 sts)*

Rnd 2: Ch 1, sk same sc as beg ch-1, 2 sc in next sc, sk next sc, 2 sc in next sc, [sk next ch, 2 sc in next ch] twice, [sk next sc, 2 sc in next sc] twice, join in first sc. *(12 sc)*

Rnds 3–5: Ch 1, sk same sc as beg ch-1, 2 sc in next sc, *sk next sc, 2 sc in next sc, rep from * around, join in first sc. At end of last rnd, fasten off.

RING FINGER
Rnd 1: With RS facing and thumb opening on left, join yarn in first sk st from Pinkie Finger, ch 1, sk same sc as beg ch-1, 2 sc in next sc, sk next sc, 2 sc in next sc, ch 2, sk next 22 sc, [sk next sc, 2 sc in next sc] twice, [sk next ch, 2 sc in next ch] twice across base of Pinkie Finger, join in first sc. *(14 sts)*

Rnd 2: Ch 1, sk same sc as beg ch-1, 2 sc in next sc, sk next sc, 2 sc in next sc, sk next ch, 2 sc in next ch, [sk next sc, 2 sc in next sc] 4 times, join in first sc.

Rnds 3–5: Ch 1, sk same sc as beg ch-1, 2 sc in next sc, *sk next sc, 2 sc in next sc, rep from * around, join in first sc. At end of last rnd, fasten off.

MIDDLE FINGER
Rnd 1: With RS facing and thumb opening on left, join yarn in first sk st from Ring Finger, ch 1, sk same sc as beg ch-1, 2 sc in next sc, sk next sc, 2 sc in next sc, ch 2, sk next 12 sc, 2 sc in next sc, [sk next sc, 2 sc in next sc] twice,

(sk next ch, 2 sc in next ch) across base of Ring Finger, join in first sc. *(14 sts)*

Rnd 2: Ch 1, sk same sc as beg ch-1, 2 sc in next sc, sk next sc, 2 sc in next sc, sk next ch, 2 sc in next ch, [sk next sc, 2 sc in next sc] 4 times, join in first sc.

Rnds 3–5: Ch 1, sk same sc as beg ch-1, 2 sc in next sc, *sk next sc, 2 sc in next sc, rep from * around, join in first sc. At end of last rnd, fasten off.

INDEX FINGER
Rnd 1: With RS facing and thumb opening on your left, join yarn in first skipped st after Middle Finger, ch 1, sk same sc as beg ch-1, 2 sc in next sc, sk next sc, 2 sc in next sc] 6 times, (sk next ch, 2 sc in next ch) across base of Middle Finger, join in first sc. *(14 sts)*

Rnds 2–5: Ch 1, sk same sc as beg ch-1, 2 sc in next sc, *sk next sc, 2 sc in next sc, rep from * around, join in first sc. At end of last rnd, fasten off.

THUMB
Rnd 1 (RS): With RS facing, join yarn in corner of thumb opening, ch 1, sk same sc as beg ch-1, 2 sc in next sc, [sk next sc, 2 sc in next sc] 4 times, sc in each of next 4 chs across base of palm, join in first sc. *(14 sc)*

Rnds 2–6: Ch 1, sk same sc as beg ch-1, 2 sc in next sc, *sk next sc, 2 sc in next sc, rep from * around, join in first sc. At end of last rnd, fasten off.

RIGHT GLOVE
CUFF
Rows 1–10: Rep rows 1–10 of Cuff of Left Glove.

BUTTONHOLE PANEL
Row 1 (RS): Ch 1, working across next side in ends of rows, work 10 sc evenly sp across side, turn.

Row 2: Ch 1, sc in each sc across, turn.

Row 3: Ch 1, sc in each of first 2 sc, *ch 2 *(buttonhole made)*, sk next 2 sc, sc in each of next 2 sc, rep from * once, turn.

Row 4: Ch 2, sc in each of first 2 sc, *2 sc in next ch-2 sp, sc in each of next 2 sc, rep from * once, ch 1, working in ends of rows of Buttonhole Panel, sc in each row, working in back lps, sc in each sc of row 10 of Cuff. Do not fasten off.

BUTTON PANEL

Row 1 (WS): Ch 1, working across next side in ends of rows, work 10 sc evenly sp across, turn.

Row 2: Ch 1, sc in each sc across, turn.

Row 3: Rep row 2.

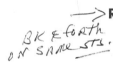

BK & forth on same sts.

Row 4: Ch 1, sc in each sc across, working across next long side of Cuff, ch 1, sc in end of each row of Button Panel, turn to RS, join in first sc at top of Button Panel.

HAND

Rnds 1–14: Rep rnds 1–14 of Hand of Left Glove.

Rnd 15: Ch 1, sk same sc as beg ch-1, 2 sc in next sc, [sk next sc, 2 sc in next sc] 8 times, ch 4, sk next 11 sc *(thumb opening made)*, 2 sc in next sc, [sk next sc, 2 sc in next sc] 7 times, join in first sc. *(38 sts)*

Rnd 16: Ch 1, sk same sc as beg ch-1, 2 sc in next sc, [sk next sc, 2 sc in next sc] 8 times, [sk next ch, 2 sc in next ch] twice, [sk next sc, 2 sc in next sc] 8 times, join in first sc. *(38 sc)*

Rnds 17–22: Rep rnd 2.

Work Fingers and Thumb same as Fingers and Thumb of Left Glove.

FINISHING

Sew buttons to Button Panel opposite buttonholes.

INFINITY SCARF

SKILL LEVEL

EASY

FINISHED MEASUREMENTS

5 x 50 inches

MATERIALS

- Cascade Yarns 220 Superwash Sport sport weight superwash wool yarn (1¾ oz/136 yds/50g per skein):
  1 skein #893 ruby
- Size K/10½/6.5mm crochet hook or size needed to obtain gauge
- Tapestry needle

GAUGE

16 sc = 4 inches; 16 rows = 4 inches

PATTERN NOTES

Weave in ends as work progresses.
Join with sl st as indicated unless otherwise stated.

SCARF

Rnd 1 (RS): Ch 200, being careful not to twist ch, **join** *(see Pattern Notes)* in first ch to form ring, ch 1, sc in same ch as beg ch-1, sc in each rem ch around, join in first sc, turn. *(200 sc)*

Rnds 2–21: Ch 1, sk same sc as beg ch-1, 2 sc in next sc, *sk next sc, 2 sc in next sc, rep from * around, join in first sc.

EDGING

Ch 2, *sl st in next st, ch 2, rep from * around, join in joining sl st. Fasten off.

With RS facing, join yarn in any st along bottom edge and work an edging round same as other edge. ■

NEW ENGLAND
Hat, Mittens & Scarf

HAT

SKILL LEVEL

EASY

FINISHED SIZE
Adult woman

FINISHED MEASUREMENTS
8½ inches long x 18 inches in circumference

MATERIALS
- Cascade Yarns 220 Superwash medium (worsted) weight superwash wool yarn (3½ oz/220 yds/100g per skein): 1 skein #1925 cobalt heather
- Size I/9/5.5mm crochet hook or size needed to obtain gauge
- Tapestry needle
- 2–2½-inch pompom maker or template

GAUGE
3 shells = 4½ inches; 9 rows = 4 inches

PATTERN NOTES
Weave in ends as work progresses.
Join with slip stitch as indicated unless otherwise stated.
Chain-3 at beginning of round counts as first double crochet unless otherwise stated.

SPECIAL STITCH
Shell: 5 dc in indicated st or sp.

HAT
BRIM
Row 1 (RS): Ch 9, sc in 2nd ch from hook, sc in each rem ch across, turn. *(8 sc)*

Rows 2–72: Ch 1, working in **back lps** *(see Stitch Guide)*, sc in each sc across, turn.

Row 73: Bring row 1 behind work, working through both thicknesses at same time, ch 1, sl st in each st across. Do not fasten off.

Turn Brim inside out so seam is on inside.

BODY & CROWN

Rnd 1: Ch 1, 72 sc evenly sp around edge of Brim, **join** (*see Pattern Notes*) in first sc.

Rnd 2: Ch 3 (*see Pattern Notes*), 3 dc in same st as beg ch-3, *sk next 2 sc, sc in next sc, sk next 2 sc, **shell** (*see Special Stitch*) in next sc, rep from * around to last 5 sc, sk next 2 sc, sc in next sc, sk last 2 sc, dc in same st as beg ch-3, join in 3rd ch of beg ch-3.

Rnd 3: Sl st in next st, ch 1, sc in same st as beg ch-1, *shell in next sc, sc in 3rd st of next shell, rep from * around to last sc, shell in last sc, join in first sc.

Rnd 4: Ch 3, 3 dc in same st as beg ch-3, *sc in 3rd st of next shell, shell in next sc, rep from * around to last shell, sc in 3rd st of next shell, dc in same st as beg ch-3, join in 3rd ch of beg ch-3.

Rnds 5–10: [Rep rnds 3 and 4 alternately] 3 times.

Rnd 11: Sl st in next st, ch 1, sc in same st as beg ch-1, *3 dc in next sc, sc in 3rd st of next shell, rep from * around to last sc, 3 dc in next sc, join in first sc. (*48 sts*)

Rnd 12: Ch 3, 2 dc in same st as beg ch-3, *sc in 2nd st of next 3-dc group, 3 dc in next sc, rep from * around to last 3-dc group, sc in 2nd st of next 3-dc group, join in 3rd ch of beg ch-3.

Rnd 13: Sl st in next st, ch 1, sc in same st as beg ch-1, *3 dc in next sc, sc in 2nd st of next 3-dc group, rep from * around to last sc, 3 dc in next sc, join in first sc.

Rnd 14: Ch 3, *sc in 2nd st of next 3-dc group, dc in next sc, rep from * around to last 3-dc group, sc in 2nd st of next 3-dc group, join in 3rd ch of beg ch-3. (*24 sts*)

Rnd 15: Ch 1, sc in each st around, join in first sc.

Rnd 16: Ch 1, **sc dec** (*see Stitch Guide*) in same st as beg ch-1 and next st, [sc dec in next 2 sts] 11 times, join in first st. (*12 sts*)

Rnd 17: Ch 1, sc dec in same st as beg ch-1 and next st, [sc dec in next 2 sts] 5 times, join in first st. Leaving long tail, fasten off. (*6 sts*)

FINISHING

With tapestry needle, weave long tail through sts of rnd 17, gather to close opening and secure.

Make a pompom using pompom maker or template and sew to top of Hat.

MITTENS

SKILL LEVEL

EASY

FINISHED SIZE

Adult woman

FINISHED MEASUREMENTS

10½ inches long x 7½ inches in circumference around palm, not including thumb

MATERIALS

- Cascade Yarns 220 Superwash medium (worsted) weight superwash wool yarn (3½ oz/220 yds/100g per skein):
    1 skein #1925 cobalt heather
- Size I/9/5.5mm crochet hook or size needed to obtain gauge
- Tapestry needle

GAUGE

3 shells = 4½ inches; 9 rows = 4 inches

PATTERN NOTES

Weave in ends as work progresses.
Join with slip stitch as indicated unless otherwise stated.
Chain-3 at beginning of round counts as first double crochet unless otherwise stated.

SPECIAL STITCH

Shell: 5 dc in indicated st or sp.

MITTEN
MAKE 2.
CUFF

Row 1 (RS): Ch 9, sc in 2nd ch from hook, sc in each rem ch across, turn. (*8 sc*)

Rows 2–28: Ch 1, working in **back lps** *(see Stitch Guide)*, sc in each sc across, turn.

Row 29: Bring row 1 behind row 28, working through both thicknesses at same time, ch 1, sc in each st across. Do not fasten off.

Turn Cuff inside out so seam is on inside.

HAND

Rnd 1: Ch 1, work 30 sc evenly sp around edge of Cuff, **join** *(see Pattern Notes)* in first sc. *(30 sc)*

Rnd 2: Ch 3 *(see Pattern Notes)*, 3 dc in same st as beg ch-3, *sk next 2 sc, sc in next sc, sk next 2 sc, **shell** *(see Special Stitch)* in next sc, rep from * around to last 5 sc, sk next 2 sc, sc in next sc, sk last 2 sc, dc in same st as beg ch-3, join in 3rd ch of beg ch-3.

Rnd 3: Sl st in next st, ch 1, sc in same st as beg ch-1, *shell in next sc, sc in 3rd st of next shell, rep from * around to last sc, shell in last sc, join in first sc, shell in next sc, join in first sc.

Rnd 4: Ch 3, 3 dc in same st as beg ch-3, *sc in 3rd st of next shell, shell in next sc, rep from * around to last shell, sc in 3rd st of next shell, dc in same st as beg ch-3, join in 3rd ch of beg ch-3.

Rnds 5–8: [Rep rnds 3 and 4 alternately] twice.

Rnd 9: Sl st in next st, ch 1, sc in same st as beg ch-1, ch 5 *(thumb opening made)*, sc in 3rd st of next shell, *shell in next sc, sc in 3rd st of next shell, rep from * around to last sc, shell in last sc, join in first sc.

Rnd 10: Ch 3, 3 dc in same st as beg ch-3, sk next 2 chs, sc in next ch, sk next 2 chs, shell in next sc, *sc in 3rd st of next shell, shell in next sc, rep from * around to last shell, sc in 3rd st of next shell, dc in same st as beg ch-3, join in 3rd ch of beg ch-3.

Rnds 11–16: [Rep rnds 3 and 4 alternately] 3 times.

Rnd 17: Rep rnd 3.

Rnd 18: Ch 3, 2 dc in same st as beg ch-3, *sc in 3rd st of next shell, 3 dc in next sc, rep from * around to last shell, sc in 3rd st of next shell, join in 3rd ch of beg ch-3. *(20 sts)*

Rnd 19: Sl st in next st, ch 1, sc in same st as beg ch-1, *sk next st, dc in next st, sk next st, dc in next st, rep from * around to last st, dc in last st, join in first sc. *(10 sts)*

Rnd 20: Ch 1, **sc dec** *(see Stitch Guide)* in same st as beg ch-1 and next st, [sc dec in next 2 sts] 4 times. Fasten off, leaving a long tail.

THUMB
Rnd 1: With RS facing, join yarn at right corner of thumb opening, ch 1, work 10 sc evenly sp around thumb opening, join in first sc. *(10 sc)*

Rnds 2–10: Ch 1, sc in each sc around, join in first sc.

Rnd 11: Ch 1, sc dec in same st as beg ch-1 and next st, [sc dec in next 2 sts] 4 times. Leaving long tail, fasten off.

FINISHING
With tapestry needle, weave long tail through sts of rnd 20 of Hand, gather to close opening and secure.

In same manner, weave long tail through sts of rnd 11 of Thumb, gather to close opening and secure.

SCARF

SKILL LEVEL

EASY

FINISHED MEASUREMENTS
5 x 60 inches, excluding fringe

MATERIALS
- Cascade Yarns 220 Superwash medium (worsted) weight superwash wool yarn (3½ oz/220 yds/100g per skein): 2 skeins #1925 cobalt heather
- Size I/9/5.5mm crochet hook or size needed to obtain gauge
- Tapestry needle
- 2–2½-inch pompom maker or template

GAUGE
3 shells = 4½ inches; 9 rows = 4 inches

PATTERN NOTES
Weave in ends as work progresses.

Chain-3 at beginning of row counts as first double crochet unless otherwise stated.

SPECIAL STITCH
Shell: 5 dc in indicated st or sp.

SCARF
Row 1: Ch 242, sc in 2nd ch from hook, sc in each rem ch across, turn. *(241 sc)*

Row 2: **Ch 3** *(see Pattern Notes)*, 2 dc in first sc, *sk next 2 sc, **shell** *(see Special Stitch)* in next sc, sk next 2 sc, sc in next sc, rep from * across to last 3 sc, sk next 2 sc, 3 dc in last sc, turn. *(40 shells)*

Row 3: Ch 1, sc in first dc, *shell in next sc, sc in 3rd st of next shell, rep from * across, working last sc in turning ch.

Row 4: Ch 3, 2 dc in first sc, *sc in 3rd st of next shell, shell in next sc, rep from * across to last shell, sc in 3rd st of last shell, 3 dc in last sc, turn.

Rows 5–12: [Rep rows 3 and 4] 4 times.

Row 13: Ch 1, sc in each st across. Fasten off. *(241 sc)*

FRINGE
Cut 10-inch strands of yarn. For each knot of Fringe, fold 4 strands in half. With crochet hook, draw folded end from WS to RS through first st on 1 short end. Draw yarn ends through folded end and pull tight. Tie 6 more Fringe knots evenly sp across end and tie 7 Fringe knots across other short end. Trim ends evenly. ■

STITCH GUIDE

STITCH ABBREVIATIONS

beg	begin/begins/beginning
bpdc	back post double crochet
bpsc	back post single crochet
bptr	back post treble crochet
CC	contrasting color
ch(s)	chain(s)
ch-	refers to chain or space previously made (i.e., ch-1 space)
ch sp(s)	chain space(s)
cl(s)	cluster(s)
cm	centimeter(s)
dc	double crochet (singular/plural)
dc dec	double crochet 2 or more stitches together, as indicated
dec	decrease/decreases/decreasing
dtr	double treble crochet
ext	extended
fpdc	front post double crochet
fpsc	front post single crochet
fptr	front post treble crochet
g	gram(s)
hdc	half double crochet
hdc dec	half double crochet 2 or more stitches together, as indicated
inc	increase/increases/increasing
lp(s)	loop(s)
MC	main color
mm	millimeter(s)
oz	ounce(s)
pc	popcorn(s)
rem	remain/remains/remaining
rep(s)	repeat(s)
rnd(s)	round(s)
RS	right side
sc	single crochet (singular/plural)
sc dec	single crochet 2 or more stitches together, as indicated
sk	skip/skipped/skipping
sl st(s)	slip stitch(es)
sp(s)	space(s)/spaced
st(s)	stitch(es)
tog	together
tr	treble crochet
trtr	triple treble
WS	wrong side
yd(s)	yard(s)
yo	yarn over

YARN CONVERSION

OUNCES TO GRAMS		GRAMS TO OUNCES	
1	28.4	25	7/8
2	56.7	40	1 2/3
3	85.0	50	1 3/4
4	113.4	100	3 1/2

UNITED STATES		UNITED KINGDOM
sl st (slip stitch)	=	sc (single crochet)
sc (single crochet)	=	dc (double crochet)
hdc (half double crochet)	=	htr (half treble crochet)
dc (double crochet)	=	tr (treble crochet)
tr (treble crochet)	=	dtr (double treble crochet)
dtr (double treble crochet)	=	ttr (triple treble crochet)
skip	=	miss

Reverse single crochet (reverse sc): Ch 1, sk first st, working from left to right, insert hook in next st from front to back, draw up lp on hook, yo and draw through both lps on hook.

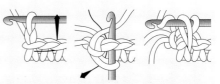

Chain (ch): Yo, pull through lp on hook.

Single crochet (sc): Insert hook in st, yo, pull through st, yo, pull through both lps on hook.

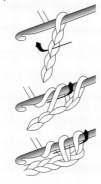

Double crochet (dc): Yo, insert hook in st, yo, pull through st, [yo, pull through 2 lps] twice.

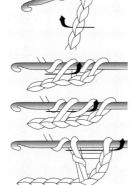

Front loop (front lp) Back loop (back lp)

Front Loop   Back Loop

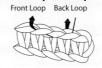

Front post stitch (fp): Back post stitch (bp): When working post st, insert hook from right to left around post of st on previous row.

Back   Front

Post of Stitch

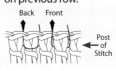

Half double crochet (hdc): Yo, insert hook in st, yo, pull through st, yo, pull through all 3 lps on hook.

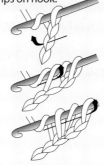

Double treble crochet (dtr): Yo 3 times, insert hook in st, yo, pull through st, [yo, pull through 2 lps] 4 times.

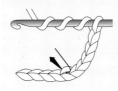

Slip stitch (sl st): Insert hook in st, pull through both lps on hook.

Chain color change (ch color change) Yo with new color, draw through last lp on hook.

Double crochet color change (dc color change) Drop first color, yo with new color, draw through last 2 lps of st.

Treble crochet (tr): Yo twice, insert hook in st, yo, pull through st, [yo, pull through 2 lps] 3 times.

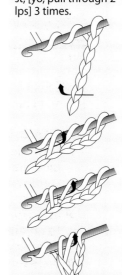

Single crochet decrease (sc dec): (Insert hook, yo, draw lp through) in each of the sts indicated, yo, draw through all lps on hook.

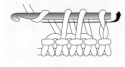

Example of 2-sc dec

Half double crochet decrease (hdc dec): (Yo, insert hook, yo, draw lp through) in each of the sts indicated, yo, draw through all lps on hook.

Example of 2-hdc dec

Double crochet decrease (dc dec): (Yo, insert hook, yo, draw lp through, yo, draw through 2 lps on hook) in each of the sts indicated, yo, draw through all lps on hook.

Example of 2-dc dec

Treble crochet decrease (tr dec): Holding back last lp of each st, tr in each of the sts indicated, yo, pull through all lps on hook.

Example of 2-tr dec

Metric
Conversion
Charts

METRIC CONVERSIONS

yards	x	.9144	=	metres (m)
yards	x	91.44	=	centimetres (cm)
inches	x	2.54	=	centimetres (cm)
inches	x	25.40	=	millimetres (mm)
inches	x	.0254	=	metres (m)

centimetres	x	.3937	=	inches
metres	x	1.0936	=	yards

INCHES INTO MILLIMETRES & CENTIMETRES (Rounded off slightly)

inches	mm	cm	inches	cm	inches	cm	inches	cm
1/8	3	0.3	5	12.5	21	53.5	38	96.5
1/4	6	0.6	5 1/2	14	22	56	39	99
3/8	10	1	6	15	23	58.5	40	101.5
1/2	13	1.3	7	18	24	61	41	104
5/8	15	1.5	8	20.5	25	63.5	42	106.5
3/4	20	2	9	23	26	66	43	109
7/8	22	2.2	10	25.5	27	68.5	44	112
1	25	2.5	11	28	28	71	45	114.5
1 1/4	32	3.2	12	30.5	29	73.5	46	117
1 1/2	38	3.8	13	33	30	76	47	119.5
1 3/4	45	4.5	14	35.5	31	79	48	122
2	50	5	15	38	32	81.5	49	124.5
2 1/2	65	6.5	16	40.5	33	84	50	127
3	75	7.5	17	43	34	86.5		
3 1/2	90	9	18	46	35	89		
4	100	10	19	48.5	36	91.5		
4 1/2	115	11.5	20	51	37	94		

KNITTING NEEDLES CONVERSION CHART

Canada/U.S.	0	1	2	3	4	5	6	7	8	9	10	10½	11	13	15
Metric (mm)	2	2¼	2¾	3¼	3½	3¾	4	4½	5	5½	6	6½	8	9	10

CROCHET HOOKS CONVERSION CHART

Canada/U.S.	1/B	2/C	3/D	4/E	5/F	6/G	8/H	9/I	10/J	10½/K	N
Metric (mm)	2.25	2.75	3.25	3.5	3.75	4.25	5	5.5	6	6.5	9.0

Annie's

Elegant, Fashionable, Chic: Accessories to Crochet is published by Annie's, 306 East Parr Road, Berne, IN 46711. Printed in USA. Copyright © 2013, 2014 Annie's. All rights reserved. This publication may not be reproduced in part or in whole without written permission from the publisher.

RETAIL STORES: If you would like to carry this pattern book or any other Annie's publication, visit AnniesWSL.com.

Every effort has been made to ensure that the instructions in this pattern book are complete and accurate. We cannot, however, take responsibility for human error, typographical mistakes or variations in individual work. Please visit AnniesCustomerCare.com to check for pattern updates.

ISBN: 978-1-59635-860-7

2 3 4 5 6 7 8 9